Communication Strategies for a Diverse World

Shusmita Sen
Angela Davis Wizner

3RD EDITION

Kendall Hunt
publishing company

Cover image © Shutterstock, Inc.

Kendall Hunt

publishing company

www.kendallhunt.com
Send all inquiries to:
4050 Westmark Drive
Dubuque, IA 52004-1840

Contents

Preface iv

Chapter 1   Getting Started as a Strategic Communicator..1

Chapter 2   Personal Communication Styles: The Strategic Communication Model 13

Chapter 3   Cultural Variation and Communication 28

Chapter 4   World View and Communication 36

Chapter 5   Communication in a Multicultural Society...45

Chapter 6   Communication in the Global Workplace 53

Chapter 7   Roadblocks to Intercultural Communication 61

Chapter 8   You, a Communication Strategist..78

Preface

Exploring diversity through the lens of communication interaction is often a challenge. This book, thus, attempts to infuse several key components to help understand the complexities of diversity. Specifically, our goal is to emphasize the "interaction" among people of different cultural backgrounds, with the intent to encourage our participants to be strategic communicators.

Committed educators, whether they be teachers in an academic setting or facilitators in the business arena, will benefit from this book, too. Any area or discipline can utilize the material in a fashion they see practical.

The book is divided into *units*, each with several sections with several objectives:

1. To allow participants to experience an intercultural concept, there are *exercises* including case studies, dyadic and group interactions, interviews, and writing components, all leading to **experiential learning**.

2. Following several exercises, a list of discussion questions are given. The questions are flexible enough to use in a variety of ways. Through discussion and sharing of ideas, this important section reinforces the intercultural exercise that participants have examined and internalized, resulting in **cognitive learning**.

3. To accompany several exercises, worksheets aimed at elaborating on the concepts are provided. Participants will be challenged to utilize **critical thinking skills** and apply what they have learned to achieve a personal perspective.

4. Lastly, each chapter is provided with a **test bank** to help reflect on the chapter content.

The various sections are necessary to provide participants with choices that meet their overall classroom/workplace objectives, taking into consideration their knowledge of diversity issues and their personal styles. The exercises and discussion questions can "stand alone"; however, for best results, one needs to delve deeper into all the sections of the book and gain individual perspectives.

Unit One offers a general look at diversity, coupled with analyses of personal communication styles.

Unit Two explores diversity in the domestic and the global arenas.

Unit Three examines the barriers in the interaction process and the causes of the breakdown in understanding others.

Unit Four provides solutions to such barriers and reach competence as a diverse **strategic communicator**.

The Authors:

The authors, with degrees in English and Communication Studies, bring both a breadth and depth to educating participants in human interactions. With extensive experience as trainers, both domestically and internationally, we hope this book helps you become an effective intercultural communicator.

Shusmita Sen: Mita.Sen@scc.spokane.edu

Angela Davis Wizner: Angela.Wizner@scc.spokane.edu

Getting Started as a Strategic Communicator

The main objective of this first chapter, besides exploring some personally-reflective exercises, is to help us realize that before we learn about others, we need to know ourselves. It is our hope that the exercises in this chapter will provide participants with opportunities to explore their own cultural attributes, become aware of their world views, and begin conversing with other participants in a group setting.

Another purpose of this chapter is to enable participants to approach the concept of Intercultural Communication hands-on, looking at the practical side of the foundational theories of cultural competencies. Through independent reflections, group activities, as well as discussion questions, participants should begin their conversations and share their personal observations.

Every little pebble in the stream believes itself to be a precious stone

-Japanese Proverb

© Feverpitch, 2008. Used under license from Shutterstock, Inc.

Sharing Personal Cultures

Objectives:

- To introduce the concept of culture
- To provide an opportunity to explore your personal culture
- To share one's personal culture with participants

Materials Needed:

- CS book: "Sharing Personal Cultures," Chapter I Exercise

Procedures:

- Complete: "Describe Your Personal Culture"
- Share your personal culture with other participants
- Record unique personal cultural elements of other participants
- Compare and contrast these unique personal cultural elements

Reflecting on personal cultural values leads to an understanding of oneself.

Sharing Personal Cultures

Describe Your Personal Culture

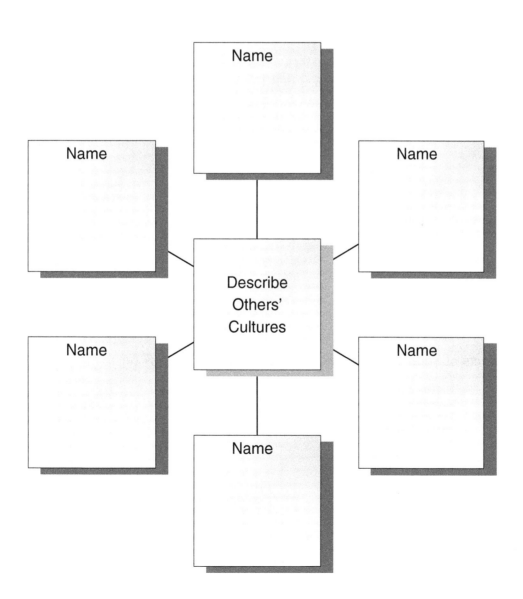

Discussion Questions

Directions:

- Complete the following questions as you examine your unique personal culture

1.   How did you describe your personal culture?

2.   What are some unique or significant aspects of others' personal cultures?

3.   What are the similarities and differences between your culture and those of others?

4.   What insights did you take away from the discussion on personal culture?

5.   What aspects of your personal culture would you like to pass on to the next generation? Why?

Finding Your Continent

To be culturally competent, we must begin by understanding the geography of our planet and discovering our place in it. The following activity will help us achieve these goals.

Objectives:

- To recognize the geography of the earth
- To identify the location of the seven continents
- To understand where we fit in this global arena

Materials Needed:

- CS book: "Find Your Continent"

Procedure:

- Label the seven continents
- Flag your own continent
- Complete the following discussion questions

Finding Your Continent

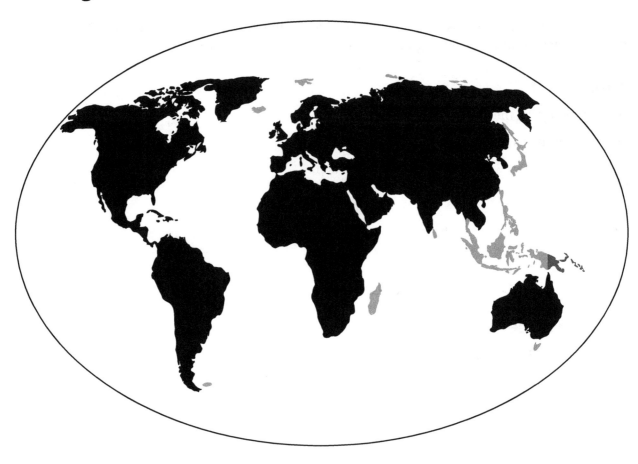

List the seven continents:

1. _____

2. _____

3. _____

4. _____

5. _____

6. _____

7. _____

Discussion Questions

1. Were you able to label each of the seven continents? Did you omit any?

2. Which continent did you label first? Why?

3. What continents surround your continent?

4. Do you have knowledge of your surrounding continents? If so, list your insights.

5. Have you traveled to any continent other than your own? Which?

The knowledge of our planetary placement assists us in discovering just how connected we are!

World Facts

Objectives:

- To introduce participants to three cultural variables that affect intercultural communication: **population, world view/religion, and world languages**
- To appreciate the richness of our planet through these culturally-diverse elements
- To experience basic research procedures

Materials Needed:

- CS book: "World Facts" and Discussion Questions
- Access to research materials: Internet, library resources, books, journals

Procedure:

- Research populations, world view/religion and world languages
- Follow-up with the discussion questions
- Upon completion, share results with participants

World Facts

Population

World population
_____

United States' population
_____

Your state's population
_____

Your city's population
_____

World View/Religion

SIX MAJOR RELIGIONS FOLLOWED GLOBALLY

1. _____   4. _____

2. _____   5. _____

3. _____   6. _____

World Languages

SIX MAJOR LANGUAGES SPOKEN GLOBALLY

1. _____   4. _____

2. _____   5. _____

3. _____   6. _____

Discussion Questions

1. How does the population of the United States compare with the world's population? With the most populated nation?

2. Do you know someone whose religion/world view differs from your own? List the differences.

3. Do you know someone whose religion/world view is similar to your own? List the similarities.

4. Do you know what language was spoken by your ancestors? Do you still speak that language today?

5. What observations did you draw from the data?

The whole world is right at our doorstep. Let us embrace all people, appreciate their unique values, and accept the gifts they bring.

Chapter 1: Test Bank

Answer the following questions to the best of your ability:

1. Why is it important to know your personal culture?

2. How would/does the knowledge help you relate to people from other cultures?

3. Why is it important to know your continent in the global context?

4. How does the population density correlate with the data from world view and languages?

5. How do you think language plays a role in culture?

6. From all the knowledge you have gained through the introductory exercises, how has your global perception changed? In what ways?

Chapter 1: Appendix

World Facts

Population

World population	7.28 billion
United States population	321.3 million
Your state's population	7.15 million
Your city's population	212,052

(Source: U.S. Census, 2015)

World view/Religion

SIX MAJOR BELIEFS/RELIGIONS GLOBALLY

1. Christianity

2. Islam

3. Hinduism

4. Buddhism

5. Sikhism

6. Judaism

Source: *Encyclopedia Brittanica*, 2015)

World Languages

SIX MAJOR LANGUAGES SPOKEN GLOBALLY

1. Mandarin

2. English

3. Hindi

4. Spanish

5. Russian

6. Arabic

(Source: dailynews.com 2015)

Personal Communication Styles: The Strategic Communication Model

This chapter will help you explore your personal verbal, nonverbal, and cultural styles, all of which are known to influence any communication interaction. Once you recognize the factors that helped shape your verbal or nonverbal styles/skills, you will learn how to adapt to others' communication patterns, which are generally quite different from yours. Once this recognition takes place, the messages can be better interpreted and less misunderstanding will result.

Verbal communication is defined as the way we use words to express ourselves. As studies show, the United States is considered a highly verbal country, and speaking directly is valued as a culture. Other countries may prefer indirect methods of speech, as demonstrated by their interaction styles.

Similarly, our nonverbal messages, such as eye contact, facial expressions, body language and other nonverbal dimensions, are also very much determined by the social and cultural influences we have had. For instance, every culture has its own sense of proximity, touch, eye movement, hand gestures, and so on. We do not always pay too close attention to these nonverbal cues unless or until we are either offended or fascinated by someone's body language or the manner of speech. Often, it is to our benefit to recognize and even acknowledge other people's verbal and non-verbal cues for better communication results, especially in a business arena.

Finally, since culture is such an integral issue in all of these, it is only natural that we try to define what it is and understand how it affects our day-to-day interactions with people around us. An extremely complex issue, culture has no single or clear-cut definition because there are several factors that help define our personal cultures. Our culture results from our family values, religious beliefs/world view, and social customs, of which we have been a part most of our lives. Culture is what gives us identity and stability in life because we belong to a certain group of people or a community or a society. As we go through the journeys of life, however, we develop other cultural attributes as necessary, especially today, participating in multicultural work environments.

As we work through these three variables, we will discover that we cannot separate them and that the three dimensions closely relate to and depend on each other in any communication effort. Because this process of communication is circular in nature, we would like to call the three elements that affect our communication styles **Verbal circle, Nonverbal circle,** and **Cultural circle.**

© Pedro Tavares, 2008. Used under license from Shutterstock, Inc.

Strategic Communication Model

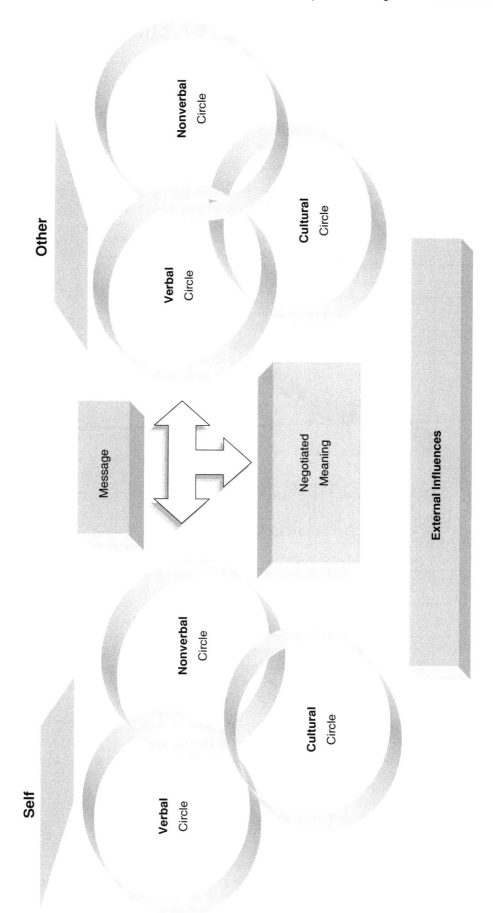

Communicating Diversity: Your Personal Interactive Style

VERBAL

_____

_____

_____

_____

NONVERBAL

_____

_____

_____

_____

CULTURAL

_____

_____

_____

_____

Discovering Your Verbal Circle

Objectives:

- To familiarize yourself with the Verbal circle of the Strategic Communication Model
- To recognize your unique verbal communication style
- To analyze your language patterns

Materials Needed:

- CS book: "Strategic Communication Model" and "Your Personal Interactive Style" circles
- Definition of Verbal circle in Chapter 2 *Appendix*, *"Strategic Communication Model: Definitions"*

Procedure:

- What language(s) do you speak? Record in the Verbal circle
- List your verbal style, using the following adjectives. The definitions are supplied for theoretical assistance:

volume	loudness or softness
pitch	voice projection: high or low
tone	inflections
rate	speed of the delivery

  Record your results in the Verbal circle
- Complete the discussion questions; share results

Discussion Questions

1.   List some of the characteristics that represent your verbal style.

2.   Do you share some of your style with a family member?

3.   Are you more or less comfortable with those that have some of the same communication characteristics as you? Why?

4.   Will your verbal style be an asset to an organization? How?

5.   Knowing your verbal circle, what challenges do you forsee?

> *Whatever words we utter*
> *should be chosen with care*
> *for people will hear them*
> *and be influenced by them for good or ill*
>
> -Buddha

Discovering Your Nonverbal Circle

Objectives:

- To familiarize yourself with the Nonverbal circle of the Strategic Communication Model
- To physically experience the use of two nonverbal cues: facial and spatial dimensions
- To compare/contrast your Nonverbal circle with others' nonverbal cues

MaterialsNeeded:

- CS book: "Discovering Your Nonverbal Circle"
- See definition of "nonverbal communication" in the Chapter 2 *Appendix*, "*Strategic Communication Model-Definitions*"

Procedure:

To help you discover your **personal space** when interacting with others

- Pick a partner
- Face one another (no furniture or "noise" between them)
- Shake hands (this represents "personal distance" in the United States)
- Touch your partner's toes with your toes, facing each other (this is the personal distance in many cultures)

Stop and De-brief:

- How did you feel when you touched toes?
- How much space do you use when interacting?
- How do we use space in the U.S.? See chart on next page for reference
- What do you know about other cultures' use of space?

Concept of Space in the United States

Distance	Category	Usage
0″–18″	Intimate	Touching; comforting
18″– 4′	Personal	Interpersonal interactions
4′–12′	Social	Business setting; formal discussions
12′+	Public	Presentations; public affairs

Adapted from: E.T. Hall, *The Silent Language* (New York: Fausett, 1959).

inue Exercise:

er your use of **eye contact** when interacting

eep the same partner

- Face each other, looking into each other's eyes while discussing a topic of choice (Direct eye contact is used in the United States)

- Look down when your partner is talking to you. (Indirect eye contact is used in several countries around the world.)

Stop and De-brief:

1. How do you feel when someone looks away or down while talking?

2. What are some of the possible reasons for varying eye contact among people?

3. What does eye contact communicate to people in the United States? Other countries?

Note: Record your use of space and eye contact in your Nonverbal circle.

We speak volumes with silence.

Discovering Your Cultural Circle

Objectives:

- To Familiarize yourself with the Cultural circle of the Strategic Communication Model
- To understand the complexity of a cultural background, but at the same time to try and come up with a broad definition of one's personal culture
- To recognize **culture** as a dynamic entity

1. Our basic or dominant culture develops from our family values, religious beliefs, and social customs, which we have been a part of most of our lives. It gives us identity and stability in life.
2. Our personal and unique culture develops and is modified with the knowledge we gain through our journey of life and the experiences we collect in the process.
3. Our personal culture is also determined by the way we perceive, interpret, and judge the world around us.

Materials Needed:

- CS book: See definition of "culture" (above) and "Discussion and Writing Assignment"

Procedures:

- Familiarize yourself with the various elements of culture
- Complete the writing assignment (by answering the questions to the best of your knowledge)
- Discussion: cultural differences and similarities

Discussion and Writing Assignment

Questions for the Writing Assignment:

Reflect on the specificities of your personal culture:

1. If you could define or describe yourself in one sentence, what would you say?

2. Where do you come from? (The place you were born in: a rural or an urban community? Your neighborhood?)

3. Did you grow up in a nuclear family or an extended family?

4. What kind of family values had you acquired while growing up?

5. What is the extent of your educational background?

6. Do you have any other hobbies, musical interests, or interests in sports?

7. How extensively have you traveled? Would you like to travel abroad if given a chance? Where would you like to go and why?

8. How many different kinds of people—different ethnicities or races—do you know? Are they mere acquaintances or good friends?

Chapter 2: Test Bank

A. Short Answers:

1. Draw the Strategic Communication Model, labeling its parts.

2. What does your Verbal circle say about your communication style?

3. Discuss the complexities of culture by providing a definition.

4. How do dyads reach understanding? Use your model to explain.

B. True or False?

1.   Personal space is similar across cultures.

2.   Direct eye contact is favored in the United States.

3.   Japanese shake hands, similar to Americans, when greeting.

4.   You should not have to adjust your communication style when sharing a message with someone from a culture different than yours.

Your Personal Journey:
Dynamic . . . ever changing . . . adapting.

Chapter 2: Appendix

Strategic Communication Model Definitions

Verbal Circle:

- The way we use language to express ourselves verbally
- The use of language symbols that are shared by a group of people

Nonverbal Circle:

- Using other methods of expression, to communicate
- These methods include the way we touch, look, smell, and use space and time

Cultural Circle:

- Unique guide for a group of people: their beliefs and values
- These belief and value systems create meaning in a society

3

Cultural Variation and Communication

From early in life, we learn to develop our personal expectations—based on our exposures to the cultural and social conditioning—and these expectations or patterns shape our perception of the world around us. Sometimes we are willing to adapt to and accept the differences in cultural and social attributes, and sometimes we refuse to see things any other way but our own. To be effective communicators, however, it is necessary to recognize those differences and reflect on our perceptions of them as we prepare ourselves for an effective interpersonal or intercultural relationship.

Specifically, different cultures practice different communication styles, not just in language but also in the *ways* that people express themselves. Geert Hofstede, a leading scholar in the field of intercultural understanding and someone who performed extensive studies on cultural patterns, concluded that there are several cultural "dimensions" or "variables" that may affect people's communication styles. The two that we will examine in this chapter are Power Distance and Individualism/Collectivism.

The case studies, which illustrate Hofstede's variables, will provide actual interactions as evidence to Hofstede's findings.

© Jan Martin Will, 2008. Used under license from Shutterstock, Inc.

Cultural Variations: Power Distance

Objectives:

- To introduce cultural variations found in every culture
- To apply the theory of cultural variations in the following case studies

Materials Needed:

- CS book: Chapter 3, Case Studies: "The Waiter" and "The Trip to the Conference"
- Outline of "Cultural Variations: Power Distance": *Chapter 3 Appendix*

Procedures:

- Read the following case studies
- Complete the discussion questions relating to the cases
- Apply Hofstede's theory on cultural variability: power distance and collectivism/individualism
- Summarize the main points, using the "Cultural Variations: Characteristics" in *Chapter 3 Appendix,* as a de-briefing tool

THE WAITER

Suzanne and her new date, Joseph, were enjoying dinner at a lovely sidewalk café. While surveying the view, Suzanne heard a tapping on a glass, only to look up and see Joe using his spoon to call the waiter, demanding service NOW! The irritated waiter, gazing at Joe, appeared at the table promptly. "Hey, I need a knife," said Joe. The waiter silently walked away, returning promptly with a knife.

Suzanne became quite embarrassed for the waitperson, while Joe commented, "I expect him to act like a waiter. He can't even do that."

Discussion Questions

1. In this actual interaction, how did Joseph view the waitperson?

2. Did Joseph communicate authority (power distance)? How?

3. Were Joseph's actions appropriate, given his culture (U.S.)?

4. What role could Suzanne have played in this situation?

5. Have you ever found yourself in a similar situation? What was your response, if any?

THE TRIP TO THE CONFERENCE

Sonia Gulati, a newly hired faculty at a four-year college, found herself in a fix. As a fresh hire, she considered herself privileged enough to be hand-picked for a trip to a National Conference for the Humanities in San Francisco with Dr. William Smith, Dean of Liberal Arts. The only problem is that being a woman from India, she is somewhat uncomfortable about going on this week-long trip, leaving her two children and her husband behind. She gathers enough courage and presents her problems to Dan Fraizer, one of her colleagues in the department. Dan looks at her directly and says, "To be professionally competent and competitive in the work force, you may have to commit to more demanding situations. Your family may not always come first. So forget about your family for a week and get ready to travel." Although a casual remark, the conversation makes Sonia somewhat nervous about the expectations. On one hand, she cannot brush aside her family's needs; on the other hand, she is aware that saying "I am sorry, I can't do that" may displease her supervisor. Unwillingly, she agrees to make this trip to San Francisco, despite all her discomfort, so as not to appear "unprofessional" or "non-Western."

Discussion Questions

1. In this interaction, how does Dan "view" Sonia?

2. Is Dan's advice to Sonia sincere and honest? Explain.

3. How would Sonia interpret Dan's reaction? Explain.

4. Was Sonia's discomfort expected, given her culture (Indian)?

5. Has a similar scenario happened to you or someone you know?

Our misconceptions and our misunderstandings
often result from our expectations that everyone thinks like us,
behaves like us, and feels like us.
Accept "differences" for better interactions
and smoother interrelations!

Chapter 3: Test Bank

Multiple Choice: Please select the single best answer in each category

1. People who live in extended families and emphasize harmony are considered:
   a. An individualistic culture
   b. A collective culture
   c. A competitive culture
   d. None of the above

2. Competitive, goal-oriented societies focus more on:
   a. Masculine traits
   b. Feminine traits
   c. Synergistic traits
   d. All of the above

3. According to Hofstede, organizations that rely on hierarchical structures are probably utilizing:
   a. Low power distance
   b. High structuralism
   c. High power distance
   d. None of the above

4. The culture dimensions that best represent the United States include:
   a. Individualism, high power, high feminine
   b. Collectivism, high power, masculine
   c. Individualism, masculine, low power
   d. Individualism, high uncertainty, high power

5. Intercultural misconceptions arise from:
   a. Inaccurate perceptions of other
   b. Thinking that all are like us
   c. Believing all feel the way we do
   d. All of the above

Chapter 3: Appendix

Cultural Variations: Characteristics

Adapted from G. Hofstede (1984)

High-Power Distance	Low-Power Distance
• Clear hierarchy established	• Less hierarchy favored
• Unequal power expected	• Equal power is expected
• Status and rank important	• Decision making is shared
• Rigid value system	• Roles are fluid
• Centralized organizational power	• Decentralized organizational structure

Collectivism	Individualism
• Community is emphasized	• Individual is the center of society
• "Face talk" is considered harmonious	• "Straight talk" is valued
• Group/family achievement is honored	• Individual achievement is important
• Cooperation is favored	• Privacy is expected
• Loyalty to one's family and company	• Loyalty to many organizations one's life time is preferred

High Uncertainty Avoidance	Low Uncertainty Avoidance
• Ambiguity is uncomfortable	• Ambiguity is comfortable
• Formal roles are necessary	• Less structure favored
• Differences are discouraged	• Differences are tolerated
• Higher stress levels are present	• Risk taking more present
• Hierarchical decision making is important	• Decision making is shared

Masculine	Feminine
• Male-oriented society	• Nurturing-oriented society
• Money and things important	• People and environment important
• Rights of men and women differ	• Sexual equality is expected
• Competition is respected	• Cooperation is valued
• Task takes precedence over relationships	• Relationships take precedence over task

Note: The United States' Profiles are as follows:

Individualism	: 91/100 (World average: 55)
Masculinity	: 62/100 (World average: 43)
Power Distance	: 40/100 (World average: 64)
Uncertainty Avoidance	: 46/100 (World average 45)

For a more comparative analysis, please refer to Hofstede's website: www.geert-hofstede.com

4

World View and Communication

In this chapter, we will address "Worldview" or "world view," a foundation based on a culture's views on religion, philosophy, humanity, and nature, among other elements. Our primary culture is formed by the social training we received in moral and ethical values during our formative years. Because these lessons are so ingrained in our subconscious mind, we do not even question why we behave in a certain way or perform certain activities or how we perceive the world around us, including the people in it. Hypothetically, for instance, it could be easier for a Tibetan to renounce materialistic life if from early childhood days he or she had been taught to do so. As emphasized in the previous chapters, knowing ourselves and our "world view" will help us develop an awareness of others' "world view" so as to build up a better understanding and more productive communication situations, especially in our diverse world today.

In the heart of a culture's "world view" lie religious and philosophical approaches to life. Acquiring knowledge of the similarities and differences in religious principles creates mindfulness in our communication interactions. Thus, world view should be an integral part of the Cultural circle of the Strategic Communication Model.

Most religions have some basic premises: one or more divine concepts; a deity or religious figure, worthy of worship; a "scripture," defining or codifying the ethical rules; spiritual leaders, to guide the followers; unique rituals and prayers. The philosophical perspective offer many of these same elements, as well as others. Both religion and philosophy offer a sense of identity or belonging. This chapter will provide you with some concepts/definitions of major world religions and help you develop an awareness and appreciation for them through activities and exercises.

World View

Objectives:

- To familiarize yourself with some of the major world religions
- To explore the similarities and the differences between religious beliefs

Materials Needed:

- CS book: Chapter 4 case study "Holy Cow!"
- Chapter 4 Appendix, "Major World Views"

Procedures:

- Discuss the assumptions and probable misconception in the case study
- Share results of the definitions and the cultural characteristics, using the chapter 4 appendix for overview Hinduism.

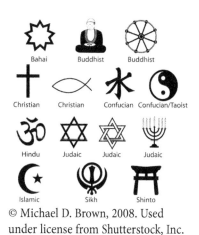

© Michael D. Brown, 2008. Used
under license from Shutterstock, Inc.

"HOLY COW!"

At a parent-teacher's meeting in Central-Valley Elementary School, the subject of food is brought up. The school is trying to make some changes in the lunch menu and, instead of serving hamburgers, the school officials suggest that more veggies would be a better option. Several parents argue that if such a drastic change is made, many children will be unhappy and perhaps even refuse to eat at school. That means the working parents would now have to pack lunches, which, in turn, would be more hassle and time-consuming.

Some parents, on the other hand, are pleased with the announcement, especially Mrs. Narayan who is a staunch Hindu from South India. She has lived in the States for the last twenty years, but she has remained a strict vegetarian all her life, as have her husband and their eleven-year old daughter. Mrs. Narayan is very happy that the school board has finally come to some sense. She blurts out, "I was always very apprehensive about my daughter eating lunch at the school cafeteria because, although she knows not to eat hamburgers or any other form of meat, it is quite possible that there would be beef stock in certain food items, which she might not know about. Back in India," she emphasizes, "we would not even let a person who eats beef into our houses. They are considered untouchables and not allowed to cross our threshold." There is pin-drop silence around the room.

Discussion Questions

Directions: Using the tenets of Hinduism listed below, discuss the following:

1.   What is the meaning behind not eating meat for Mrs. Narayan?

2.   Why were the other participants taken aback by her comment?

3.   What solution would you have proposed to meet Mrs. Narayan's concerns and those who do not follow her concerns?

Elements of Hinduism

Note: We have included key principles of Hinduism to assist you with this case study

- Since all life forms are sacred, eating flesh, particularly beef, is prohibited and strictly rejected by many Hindus
- Cows are considered a symbol of motherhood because of their milk
- In the ancient aggrarian society, slaughtering of cows was prohibited in the Hindu scriptures and frowned upon by society as a whole
  - Mrs. Narayan expressed her staunch Hindu views; our awareness of her three circles should lead to negotiated meaning
  - According to the polytheistic doctrine, meant for the common people, all natural forms—the sun, the moon, the earth, air, water, and all life forms—are worthy of worship and to be kept contented, so that they do not bring pain, misfortunes, and destructions.
  - Since all life forms are sacred, eating flesh is prohibited and strictly rejected by many Hindus.

World View Worksheet

Judaism

- Key leaders/deities:

  _____

- Sacred writings:

  _____

- Key Principles:

  1. _____

  2. _____

  3. _____

Christianity

- Key leaders/deities:

  _____

- Sacred writings:

  _____

- Key principles:

  1. _____

  2. _____

  3. _____

Islam

- Key leaders/deities:

  _____

- Sacred writings:

  _____

- Key principles:

  1. _____

  2. _____

  3. _____

Hinduism

- Key Leaders/Deities:

  _____

- Sacred Writings:

  _____

- Key Principles:

  1. _____

  2. _____

  3. _____

Buddhism

- Key Leaders/deities:

  _____

- Sacred writings:

  _____

- Key principles:

  1. _____

  2. _____

  3. _____

Confucianism

- Key Leaders/deities:

  _____

- Sacred writings:

  _____

- Key principles:

  1. _____

  2. _____

  3. _____

Chapter 4: Test Bank

Multiple Choice: **Please *select the single best answer***

1. The book of sacred scriptures for Muslims is called:

    a. The Holy Bible

    b. The Quran

    c. The Upanishads

    d. The Analects

2. The Savior for Christian followers is:

    a. Brahman

    b. Abraham

    c. Jesus

    d. Ganesh

3. Believing in one God is considered:

    a. Monotheistic

    b. Polytheistic

    c. Dualistic

    d. Non-fatalistic

4. A person's view on religion, philosophy, nature, among other elements, is termed:

    a. Verbal view

    b. World view

    c. Tunnel view

    d. None of the above

5. Similarities found in religions include:

    a. The use of rituals

    b. Prayer

    c. A sacred book or collection of writings

    d. All of the above

Chapter 4: Appendix

Major World Views

Religion	Deities/Key Leaders	Sacred Writings	Key Principles
Judaism	Yahweh	Torah in Hebrew Bible	God's chosen people; God is one; no human will ever be divine
Christianity	God (The Trinity: Father, Son, and Holy Spirit)	Holy Bible	Jesus is the Savior; two greatest commandments, Love God and Love neighbor as yourself
Islam	Allah	Quran	Five Pillars of Practice: fasting, almsgiving, pilgrimage, creed, prayer
Hinduism	Brahma, Vishnu, Shiva	Upanishads and the Bhagwat Gita	Divine in every thing; dharma, a way of life; multiple paths
Buddhism	Buddha	The Pali Canon	Four Noble Truths; the Eightfold Path; overcoming suffering leads to Nirvana
Confucianism	Confucius	Analects	Social, political, and ethical concepts inspired by Confucius' teachings

Note: Above are concise summaries of world views; continue research and find out more!

Communication in a Multicultural Society

One place where cultural diversity plays a significant role today is the workplace. Everyday at work, we meet people from various walks of life. Whether it is someone from China or Belarus or someone from the suburbs or the valley, we are sure to find ourselves in a communication situation where we are expected to behave or interact in a certain way so as to be **mindful.** According to Buddhism, mindfulness takes into consideration the communication style of others. Without this awareness, we are sure to offend someone inadvertently. Our success in relationships in the workplace, therefore, depends on how well we can adapt to various communication situations.

The United States is one nation in which people from diverse nationalities, ethnicities, and racial profiles have made their home, and they have all become members of what we call **domestic co-cultures.** Every cultural group value systems, unique religious beliefs, social customs, food habits and cultural ceremonies. Consequently, people from various co-cultures demonstrate typical (often different from those of the dominant culture) verbal and nonverbal communication patterns. Although we should refrain from stereotyping, a Japanese- American co-worker, for example, may not look directly in the eye when communicating in a power distance setting; or an immigrant from a Slavic community may constantly apologize for his or her lack of sufficient English vocabulary skills. These differences, understandably, may lead to confusions, misunderstandings, stereotyping, and frustration.

As members of this multicultural society, we should consider some facts. First, history shows us that every one of these cultural groups has helped add a different color or a unique thread to rich tapestry of the "American culture." Second, with the cacophony of sounds, accents, language skills, and complexities of verbal and nonverbal styles, it is the people from diverse backgrounds who have made the United States a cultural bouillabaisse.

This chapter will help participants see how diverse America is today. Through a few research activities, you will learn about the cultural demographics–the people we meet and interact with on any given day. Knowledge of a few cultural variables will also help resolve uncertainties in communication problems and help raise tolerance among the communicators, especially in a workplace setting.

*People from other parts of the world bring
their unique verbal styles, their sense of
time, space, and touch. There is always something we can learn
from such diversity!*

© Lorelyn Medina, 2008. Used under license from Shutterstock, Inc.

Communication and American Idioms

Objectives:

- To understand commonly used idioms and their relevance in the workplace in the United States
- To explore translations and their effect on decoding messages, which may otherwise lead to a failed communication interaction
- To discover the complexities of the Verbal circle

Materials Needed:

- CS book: "Some Common American Idioms"

Procedures:

- Review the idioms listed for their meaning
- Illustrate the idioms by using them in sentences
- Share answers, utilizing the correct definitions/translations

Some Common American Idioms

Idioms	Translations
1. "Lay it on thick"	Flatter somebody, often for personal gain
2. "Bad mouth"	Unflattering, unkind words
3. "Savvy"	Knowledgeable about something
4. "Piece of cake"	To be very easy
5. "Out of line"	Impolite, disrespectful, disregarding rules or protocol
6. "Live wire"	A highly-energetic person
7. "Pull an all-nighter"	Study or work all night
8. "Break a leg"	Good luck!
9. "Cut a deal"	Reach an agreement
10. "Beats me!"	No idea

Directions

After reviewing the idioms and their meanings above, create sentences out of each idiom, showing their relevance in a work/business context. For example, "We need to cut a deal or the stockholders will lose their investment." Use extra space if necessary.

1. _____

2. _____

3. _____

4. _____

5. _____

6. _____

7. _____

8. _____

9. _____

10. _____

Understanding Work Place Co-Cultures

Objectives:

- Explore the ethnic diversity that make up the montage of the U.S. population
- To be prepared for a montage of colleagues in ther U.S. work place

Materials Needed:

- CS book "U.S. Census: Ethnic Populations"

Procedures:

- Research current data on U.S. ethnic populations using U.S. Census
- Share results with participants

© Andresr, 2008. Used under license from Shutterstock, Inc.

U.S. Census: Ethnic Populations

Ethnic Co-Culture	Estimate
American Indian & Alaska Native	
Asian	
Black or African American	
Hispanic or Latino	
Native Hawaiian & other Pacific Islanders	
White	
Other	

Knowing Your Co-Worker

Objectives:

- Understanding the culture-specific elements reflected in a person's verbal and nonverbal communication styles, especially for someone from a cultural background that is different from one's own

- Developing awareness of others' Verbal, Nonverbal, and Cultural circles; the purpose is to help adapt to other's communication styles

Procedures:

- Brainstorm with a co-worker who is a member of a different co-culture from your own

- Answer the following questions and share your perceptions with others

Assignment Guidelines:

1. Choose a co-worker or an aquaintance from a different cultural group than your own

2. Research as many unique and typical cultural attributes and communication patterns of this ethnic group

3. Write an essay summarizing your findings to illustrate a detailed profile of this group's verbal and nonverbal communication patterns

    - Some areas of interest might be their use of space or eye contact and body language; their sense of time; the speed and clarity of their speech and their speech pattern

4. In your essay, include a few strategies that you would use to interact with this person at a workplace setting to avoid uncertainties or unpleasant situations with verbal and nonverbal communication

ExtraQuestion: Are the verbal and nonverbal cues of this person similar to or different from yours? Explain with evidence?
Discuss with participants

Chapter 5: Test Bank

1. Approximately how many different ethnic groups can you easily identify as living in the United States?

2. Which ethnic co-culture has the largest population in the United States?

3. Which ethnic co-culture has the smallest population in the United States?

4. Do you know someone from any of the co-cultures listed above? What are their *nonverbal* and *verbal* characteristics? (Use census website for specifics to couple with your own experiences)

5. Provide a commonly used idiom today and show its relevance in an interaction (do not use idioms in the list above)

Communication in the Global Workplace

Now that you are aware of different cultural values of the people we live or work with in the United States, it is time for us to extend our vision further into the International business arena. As we speak, America is developing more and more business relationships with countries from around the world. Today, our late-night inquiries on any computer issues are being answered by someone outside the U.S.; our health records are being managed by companies in Malaysia; and, of course, our clothes and other commodities are being manufactured in China and Bangladesh.

A greater number of Americans are traveling to other parts of the world not only as tourists but as delegates of the American workforce to make lucrative business deals. If it is hard to communicate without any hitch with co-cultures living in our own neighborhood, think of how much more complex and confusing it would be to communicate with people living in foreign countries. English, in a great many countries, is NOT the language of conversation! Also, some of the nonverbal elements would be much more pronounced in cultures outside the United States, which could easily raise the levels of uncertainties and discomfort.

As you go through this chapter, several cultural idiosyncrasies will be apparent; they are characteristics that are unknown to us or sometimes even overlooked. Such a wide array of cultural practices must be continually researched. We, therefore, encourage you to explore specific and common communication patterns of a nationality if you are planning a trip to that particular country. This way, you can avoid surprises and/or unpleasant situations.

GLOBAL COMMUNICATION: The Nonverbal Arena

Objectives:

- To understand the dynamics of communication in the international setting
- To explore the Nonverbal circle of communication through touch and the use of space
- To apply and share analysis of the case study

Materials Needed:

- CS book: Chapter 6 case study "To Each His Own"
- CS book: "Concept of Space in the United States," *Chapter 6 Appendix*

Procedures:

- Discuss the concept of space and proximity reflected in the following case study
- Share results with others and de-brief, using the information from the *Appendix*, "Concept of Space in the United States"

TO EACH HIS OWN!

Paul McDonald is sent by his company, Cyber Intelligence, to Florence, Italy, for a prospective business relationship with Santoro Software Development. Upon arrival, he is greeted by Marcello Capelleni, the local company representative at the airport. This new acquaintance is very warm and friendly, as he bellows greetings and extends his hand for a strong and sure handshake. Paul feels at ease immediately and looks forward to the next few days in this foreign land.

Later that evening, a party is held at the CEO's house to welcome Paul, and despite his jet lag, Paul feels it necessary to comply since he is here on a lucrative business proposition and does not want to offend anyone.

Marcello picks up Paul from his hotel around 6:30 and fills him in with names of people, their positions in the company, including little gossips, etc. At the party, Marcello offers to introduce his new acquaintance to the executives, grabs his hand, and takes him around the room, equally enthusiastic and loud. Throughout the meetings, however, Paul is aware that Marcello does not let go of his hand, and as the evening progresses, the grasp gets stronger and stronger. Paul finds his shoulders becoming tense as he begins to feel ill and decides to turn in early.

DISCUSSION QUESTIONS

1. Why is Paul feeling ill?

2. Compare and contrast Paul and Marcello's Nonverbal circles. Include in your answer the Strategic Communication Model.

3. In a similar situation, how would you negotiate meaning between you and a co-worker?

THE INTERNATIONAL BUSINESS ARENA: The Strategic Communication Model

Objectives:

- To be informed of the top ten trading partners of the United States
- To research and apply the statistical information to one of these countries
- To create a business brief, including the communication patterns of the country of choice
- To be aware of the importance of intercultural communication, specifically **verbal, nonverbal,** and **cultural** dimensions, while interacting with international business partners

Materials Needed:

- CS book: Chapter 6, "U.S. International Trading Partners" and "Communication and the International Business Arena" with the "Business Brief"
- Internet/library access for research

Procedures:

- Research and complete the chart on "U.S. International Trading Partners" incorporating the sums of the value of imports and exports in U.S. dollars
- Choose a country from the list of the U.S top ten trading partners and research it, specifically regarding their communication style
- Complete "Business Brief"
- Share your findings with others

Business Brief

Country of Business: _____

Ethnic Population(s) of Country: _____

Verbal characteristics to consider in a business interaction:

Language/s spoken and written: _____

Nonverbal characteristics to consider in a business interaction:

- Time usage:

  _____

- Eye contact:

  _____

- Space usage:

  _____

- Use of touch:

  _____

- Clothing:

  _____

Cultural Variables to consider (religion, history, masculine/feminine characteristics, collective/individual families, modesty, etc.):

_____

_____

_____

U.S INTERNATIONAL TRADING PARTNERS

Country	Sum of the Value of Imports and Exports in U.S. Dollars
1. Canada	
2. Mexico	
3. Japan	
4. China	
5. Federal Republic of Germany	
6. United Kingdom	
7. Republic of Korea	
8. France	
9. Taiwan	
10. Italy	

One bows, one kisses, one loves silence, one loves to share! Are you ready to do business in the 21st century?

Chapter 6: Test Bank

Answer the questions to the best of your ability:

1. Personal space in the United States is measured at:

    a. 0 inches–12 inches

    b. 0 inches–25 inches

    c. 18 inches–4 feet

    d. 4 feet–12 feet

2. In the case study, "To Each His Own," Paul probably felt ill because:

    a. He had the flu

    b. His space and touch were invaded

    c. He did not speak Italian

    d. None of the above

3. Trading partners for the United States include:

    a. Mexico

    b. Canada

    c. China

    d. All of the above

4. When conducting business outside of the United States, one should consider:

    a. The country's use of time

    b. The country's use of space

    c. The country's use of touch

    d. All of the above

5. The United States' largest trading partner is:

    a. Canada

    b. Mexico

    c. Argentina

    d. None of the above

Chapter 6: Appendix

© Sabri Deniz Kizil, 2008. Used under license
from Shutterstock, Inc.

Roadblocks To Intercultural Communication

7

In the United States, people from all walks of life enjoy religious, social, and political freedom; where citizens are promised "life, liberty, and the pursuit of happiness." So, what is the need for "diversity training"? Are we obsessed with having to be politically correct because society expects us to be so? One logical explanation might be that despite our conscious and continuous efforts to understand and appreciate cultural differences, we still run into "roadblocks." No matter how much we would like to believe that we are free from bigotry, there are still instances of stereotypes, prejudices, biases, and discriminations, including racism, ageism, and homophobia.

In our interactions with people from other cultural, racial, and social groups, many of us cannot always ignore the obvious differences between "us" and "them." There is often the issue of language barrier when we are verbally interacting with people from other parts of the world. At times, there is a sense of hesitation when we are faced with an individual who has a unique accent, an unfamiliar body language, or a "peculiar" dress code. We may even halt for a moment every time we see different skin color or facial features. Such attitudes or feelings result from "ethnocentrism"—the belief that our own culture, whichever it might be, is superior to other cultures.

Ethnocentrism is a natural and inevitable process, its seeds often planted in us through generations. It is nurtured by negative experiences due to personal conflicts with members of other racial or cultural groups, and it is kept alive through negative social conditionings. Most of these attitudes, unfortunately, are based on insufficient knowledge and lack of sensitivity. This chapter will help you discover the causes and the effects of these roadblocks and show you how to rise above our ethnocentrism and become strategic communicators in the intercultural arena. The bottom line is:

We need to be honest with ourselves and work from inside out.

Roadblocks to Strategic Communication

Objectives:

- To understand the language of stereotype, prejudice, and discrimination
- To research these three areas, identifying distinctions between them
- To explore the prevalence of discrimination in America today

Materials Needed:

- CS book: "Definition of Terms" and *Chapter 7 Appendix* "Roadblocks to Strategic Communication"

Procedures:

- Using the CS book, research the three concepts listed on "Definition of Terms," including examples/stories representing each term
- Discuss definitions; after the definitions have been established, discuss examples/stories to illustrate the concepts
- As you discuss these issues (see questions below for assistance), distinguish differences among the three terms

Definition of Terms

Stereotyping:

- Definition:

- Examples:

Prejudice:

- Definition:

- Examples:

Discrimination:

- Definition:

- Examples:

Discussion Questions

1.   What are the definitions for stereotyping, prejudice, and discrimination?

2.   How has your background or experiences contributed to your attitudes about people different from you?

3.   How widespread is the problems of stereotyping, etc. in your family? Neighborhood?

4.   What would be your response if you saw an act of discrimination taking place?

5.   What can be done to fight discrimination?

6.   Have you ever experienced discrimination personally? Would your life be different if you did not have to deal with this reality?

Roadblocks are the perceptual barriers that inhibit our communication process!

Cultural Recognition and Stereotyping

Objective:

- To develop awareness of cultural diversity in every walk of life
- To examine cultural stereotyping

Materials Needed:

- CS book: "Cultural Recognition" and images of people

Procedures:

- In groups, discuss the possible country of origin or the ethnic or racial backgrounds of the people in the images
- List your choices under each picture; then discuss the rationale behind the choices
- Share correct answers and discuss possible stereotypes associated with identifying different racial groups (correct answers provided at end of chapter)

Directions

List either the country of origin or the ethnic or racial background under the images below. Share your answers with your group, including the discussion questions that follow.

_____

_____

_____

_____

_____

_____

_____

_____

_____

Images provided by the authors.

Discussion Questions:

1. On what criteria was your choice of the country of origin based? (facial features, clothing, other cultural identifications?)

2. How accurate were your assumptions? Out of the eight images, how many could you correctly identify?

3. How did you feel if you were incorrect in your assumptions? Did stereotyping play a role?

4. How can you increase your cultural awareness? Include the Strategic Communication Model in your answer.

Agism and Communication Challenges

Objective:

- To examine the perceptions of cultures and different views on "age"
- To analyze the prejudice as a foundation for discrimination

Materials Needed:

- CS book:"Age and Communication" and "Interview Questions"

Procedures:

- Interview a person from an age group older than you
- Using the questions listed below, discuss your findings

Interview Questions

1.   What do you consider to be the age of responsibility?

2.   Is there a specific age to date? Marry?

3.   Is there a ritual or societal message involved in marking a certain age?

4.   How are the elderly viewed in your co-culture?

5.   Which of the statements below would you say best represents your view of age:

Age and Wisdom are Inseparable.
Or
There comes an age when one should bow out gracefully.

Next, justify your rationale

Uncertainty: A Model of Failure

Objectives:

- To explore any major roadblocks to effective intercultural communication
- To share with participants the "A Model of Failure"
- To apply the model to a case study

Materials Needed:

- CS book: "A Model of Failure" and the case study "My Client, Maria"

Procedures:

- Read the case study "My Client, Maria"
- Provide a protocol for Maria, including in the answer the need for an understanding of "others" and their three circles; complete discussion questions and share with participants
- Review "A Model of Failure"; discuss the components in the model

A Model of Failure

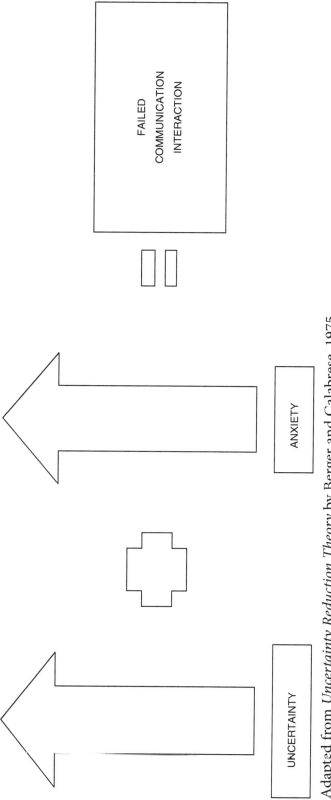

FAILED COMMUNICATION INTERACTION

ANXIETY

UNCERTAINTY

Adapted from *Uncertainty Reduction Theory* by Berger and Calabrese, 1975

My Client, Maria

On my way to my first appointment of the day!

Just this morning, I was reviewing the assessment again to get a feel for the new client assigned to me, Maria Cortez. Maria is "a first-generation Mexican American and speaks little English," it said.

Through my years of experience working as a counselor for the Department of Health, I must admit I had not had a client who did not speak English. There are enough challenges without having to work with this problem, I thought to myself.

I'll just treat her as anyone else.

_____

Your Charge
As a health employee, how can you help to make Maria's first appointment go smoothly? Provide a procedure you may utilize below. Include the client's possible three circles when considering your plan.

Procedure
Verbal:

Nonverbal:

Cultural:

Discussion Points: When reviewing this case study, discuss the Model of Failure, emphasizing that when we are confronted with a dyadic interaction, where we lack knowledge of the "other" and their three circles, we become anxious. We will thus ignore and withdraw from the interaction so as to decrease our anxiety. This response results in a failed attempt to communicate effectively. By learning Maria's three circles, we "negotiate meaning," leading to a successful communication process.

Chapter 7: Test Bank

Answer the questions to the best of your ability:

1.   Distinguish between stereotyping and prejudice. Provide an example of each.

2.   Discrimination is defined as acting on one's categorization of a group of people. Where do you see that happening in the United States today? Be specific.

3.   What variables make a communication interaction fail? Use "A Model of Failure" in your response.

4.   List three suggestions you provided for a successful interaction with "Maria" (case study: "My Client, Maria"). Consider in your answer her personal circles.

5.   Where have you personally seen discrimination take place? Describe the interaction or event specifically.

Chapter 7: Appendix

Definition of terms

Stereotypes:

- Preconceived notions about members of a culture different than our own
- "Pictures in our heads," misperceptions

Prejudices:

- Negative attitudes toward another group of people different than our own
- Conscious feeling of superiority over a particular group

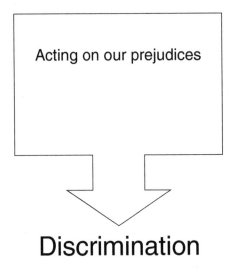

Correct Answers for Images Activity

Russia

Taiwan

Afghanistan

Kyrgyzstan

Vietnam

Iraq

Ukraine

Siberia

China

You, a Communication Strategist

In this final chapter, let us review the main elements we have covered in the book. One of the main criteria for any type of communication, definitely true for intercultural communication, is **self-awareness**. Before we try to understand others, we need to "know" ourselves. Chapters 1 through 4 present the **foundation** or building blocks on which rests your understanding of yourself in the intercultural arena. Chapter 1 helps test your basic knowledge of the world around you. Chapter 2 helps you analyze the three circles—verbal, nonverbal, and cultural—all of which affect your personal communication style. Chapters 3 and 4 reveal other cultural variations—such as whether you come from a collectivist or individualist society or how influenced are you by world views, including religious and philosophical elements—all of which help shape your personality, which in turn influences your communication patterns.

The second part of this book is the **application** of what you learned in the first unit. Just as you have certain unique qualities, some typical behavior patterns related to your verbal and nonverbal styles, other people—whether belonging to different social, cultural, and ethnic groups—possess their own qualities and their own idiosyncrasies that influence their communication styles. Instead of resisting those differences, it is in our best interest to recognize the cultural diversities and adapt to the differences, especially if we have a business relationship with people from multicultural backgrounds. Chapters 5 and 6 help us move beyond ourselves and learn about others—both in the domestic and the international arena. We now live in a global village where new doors are opening every day, new businesses, new possibilities, and new relationships are developing, making it even more necessary to adapt quickly and efficiently.

The new possibilities may not always erase old habits, and challenges—both old and new—may sometimes negatively impact our communication efforts. It is, therefore, essential to learn what causes negative emotions that prevent us from accepting other readily. Chapter 7 provides insight into what keeps us from treating others with the same respect as we would like to be treated with.

Finally, this last chapter will help bring all of the elements of intercultural communication into perspective. Through a few relevant activities, you will be able to evaluate your abilities as a strategic communicator. Practice the key elements of intercultural communication you picked up from this workbook and be confident with your interactions with others among us!

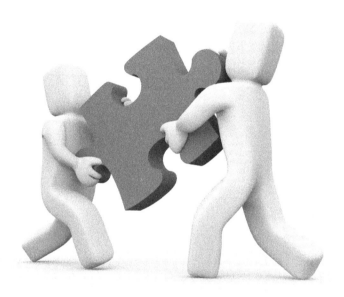

© Palto, 2008. Used under license from Shutterstock, Inc.

Strategic Skills for Effective Intercultural Communication

Objectives:

- To explore various skills one can utilize when communicating interculturally
- To be able to utilize these skills in an intercultural interaction
- To become a strategic communicator

Materials Needed:

- CSG workbook: "Strategic Skills for Effective Intercultural Communication" and "Using Strategic Skills: Practice Scenarios" worksheet
- "Strategic Skills" model

Procedures:

- Display the "Strategic Skills" model, emphasizing choices we have when interacting in the intercultural arena.
- Emphasize the need for one or several approaches, depending on the culture in which you are negotiating.
- Have the participants practice their communication by completing the "Practice Scenarios" worksheet.
- Review the worksheet (perhaps role play the scene), analyzing the strengths and weaknesses of the choices; discussion questions, as well.
- Emphasize the need to be "strategic" in their choices to achieve a successful interaction.

Strategic Skills Model

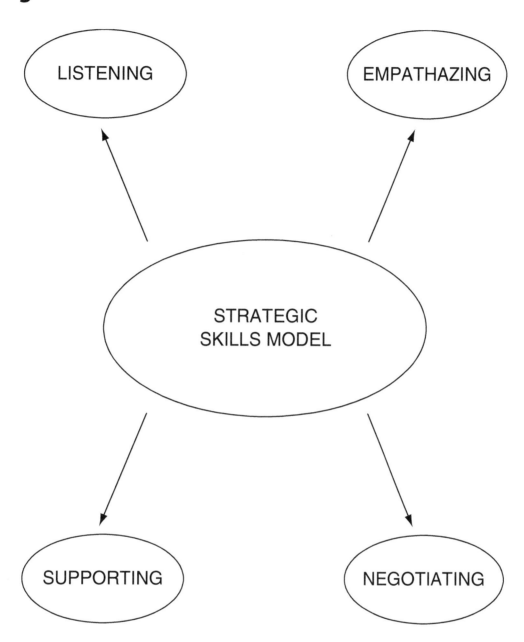

Using Strategic Skills: Practice Scenarios

1. A co-worker of yours, Mr. Yakamoto, asks you for your opinion on his proposal. How should you best respond?

    Listening statement: So, you would like a little input?

    Empathy statement: It sounds like a lot of your energy went into this.

    Supporting statement: This looks solid!

    Negotiating statement: It's great! I like the summary and perhaps if an introduction was added to your solid summary, that would do it.

Considerations: Japanese are face-saving participants ("other's face") in an interaction, thus you would also want to save his face. Though he asked for input, evaluating it specifically may embarrass him, thus a comment or two would suffice. Focus on the remaining skills for a successful intercultural interaction.

2. Jose Cortez is manager of a large industrial plant in Mexico. His purchasing orders for the United States are lagging behind. A representative from a U.S. company has called Jose on the phone. What is the best communication approach to take with Mr. Cortez?

    Listening statement:

    _____

    Empathy statement:

    _____

    Supporting statement:

    _____

    Negotiating statement:

    _____

Considerations:

| |
| |
| |
| |
| |

Walking the Walk

Objectives:

- To assist participants in becoming an intercultural communication researchers
- To collect and analyze nonverbal data
- To understand the importance of nonverbal communication, specifically kinesics (clothing)

Materials Needed:

- CSG workbook "Walking the Walk," "Experiment Observation Sheet," and "Research Evaluation Sheet," as well as artifacts from other cultures, such as clothing, headwear, face paints (optional), and any objects that can be worn

Procedures:

1. Have approximately five participants wear the clothing or artifacts from other cultures (participants should volunteer for these positions).

2. Have participants wear the clothing or artifacts for 1–2 hours, either within the confines of the room or outdoors.

3. Ask remaining participants to follow obscurely, observing and noting nonverbal and verbal cues of the participant on the "Experiment Observation Sheet."

4. For the remaining time, facilitate participant discussion of their experiences using the "Walking the Walk: Data Analysis" questionnaire or any other element they'd like to share from their experiment.

Experiment Observation Sheet

Culture _____

Eye-contact

Men – (Interaction with)

None	1x	2x	3x	4x	5x

Women – (Interaction with)

None					Every time

Space/Distance From

Women – (Interaction with)

Close		1ft.		More than 2ft.

Men – (Interaction with)

Inches		2 ft.		4 ft.

Speaking Distance

Women – (Interaction with)

Smell breath away		1/2 ft. – 1 ft.		1½ ft.

Men – (Interaction with)

Walk away from				Stop and talk to

Touch

Men – (Interaction with)

None	1x	2x	3x	4x	5x

Women – (Interaction with)

None					Every time

Walking the Walk: Data Analysis

Overview

1. What nonverbal cues did you observe in your subject? Which fit your "codes" and which did not?

2. What verbal "codes" did you observe in your subject? Which fit your "codes" and which did not?

3. What did you observe about other people? Include positive and negative observations.

4. How could you have changed the project to make it more effective? Be specific.

5. What was positive about this experiment? Be specific.

6.   What emerged from the experiment that you did not expect?

7.   Does this method of measuring your learning increase your understanding of the importance of intercultural communication?

NAME:_____

Chapter 8: Test Bank

Answer the questions to the best of your ability:

1. To become commuication strategists, we need to:
   a. Know ourselves and our individual three circles
   b. Know our participants and their three circles
   c. Negotiate meaning between ourselves and others
   d. All of the above

2. When conducting business with the Japanese, which of the following strategic skills would be considered the most mindful choice?
   a. Advising, letting them know clearly what you want
   b. Supporting: saving their face and praising the idea
   c. Judging, telling them why they need to change
   d. None of the above

3. Summarize your three circles. Be specific, providing examples that clearly fit the category.

4. Choose a country in which to do business. Provide their three circles.

5. Combining questions 3 and 4, draw your three circles and the three circles of the country you chose. Describe the adjustments you may make to reach a shared understanding.

Becoming a Strategic Communicator in a Diverse World

- KNOW "SELF": YOUR PERSONAL PROFILE

- KNOW "OTHERS": INTERACTANTS' PERSONAL PROFILE

- APPRECIATE YOUR INDIVIDUAL **DIVERSITY** AND **DIVERSITY** IN OTHERS

- UTILIZE EFFECTIVE COMMUNICATION SKILLS TO CREATE **NEGOTIATED MEANING:** FITTING THE PIECES OF THE PUZZLE

© Marinini, 2008. Used under license from Shutterstock, Inc.